ISBN 979-8-9913942-0-8

Published by Hidden Hand Press
www.hiddenhandbooks.com

HIDDEN HAND PRESS

ANDROMEDA DREAMS: GREATEST HITS | POEMS | BEYOND

by Garrett Carroll
and
Hamant Singh

BY GARRETT CARROLL

BY HAMANT SINGH

Acknowledgements

GARRETT CARROLL

For Mrs. Turner. From calling letters "words" in 1st grade to writing poems brimming with words, this is the 1st from me.

HAMANT SINGH

I am grateful to my friends and family for their constant support. Special mention to the Horror Writers' Association (HWA) and the Science Fiction & Fantasy Poetry Association (SFPA) for creating a very special community. This book is dedicated to all agents of Chaos.

AMBIENT MARS

The best place to find sub-genre music
is right at its location's source,
and these colorful synthy textures
are dug up directly from the Martian dunes—
some sonorous melodies, the soul-soothing
motion of chords that drift like winds in smooth
flight,
recorded through the audio tech of the rovers
and bluetoothed to my insulated ears.

Swishing sounds ignite dream after dream
of my feet splotching the dry-soaked ground
someday, overlooking the red planet like a splinter,
stepping outside the Martian port,
watching machinations clean the air below
as they dig up more perfect songs for me;

ambient Mars and rain will be.

THE TIMEKEEPER

A senseless conductor

who keeps the absolute

precision of rhythms and notes in check

while letting forth a discordance

of disembodied soundbites

that gel and form together,

creating a layer of

untouched and unseen soundscapes

that cover every atom

of dark and light matter

flowing through the universe.

To merely feel its warmth

is to see with vivid eyes

and walk on the darkness

in the depths of space

between the stellar bodies.

THE BAND FROM ANDROMEDA

In Andromeda, they played in all kinds of venues—

in aqua-domes for six-eyed squids sloshing

their seven tentacles across sea floors,

in the stadium trunks of trees for blorgs pumping

their stubby,

elbowless arms in unison through the air,

in ecumenopolis bars for musing avians and mammals

levitating

on dusty red fabric pillows,

for the slaves self-exiled from the clubs and wars

of their origin galaxies, the new bonds of melodious

love

giving shimmers of hope sent across FTL soundwaves,

harmonies to the strands and environments

of innumerable living species.

After sweeping through Andromeda,

touring and rising to levels of unheard stardom,

the band took the risk and traveled the spiraling

bridge

to the Milky Way.

There they enchanted more crowds,

all types of people who jumped and pumped and

howled

their anatomies through the aura's air,

igniting a trillion, subatomic fiery stars to sway in

unison

from the homes—cliffs, caverns, forests, mountains,

metropolitans,

everywhere in our galaxy, all the lighters burning

bright,

swaying and swinging to the melodies and rhythms of

the soulful music.

Then the touring abruptly ceased, the band went

quiet.

Living in the unknown and unseen void beyond

the galaxies, in a forested cabin on a living asteroid,

they planned a project most ambitious in scope;

an orchestra of races coming together to create

within the most pleasing harmonic ranges, to bring
the galaxies

together truly, to link the galactic bridges through
sound.

Silence ensued, and fans clawed to the scant
discography in anticipation.

A single winking pluck, followed by a crescendo

through everyone's ears. All races, genders, and
creatures

processed the sound as the band and thousands of
interstellar musicians

swelled into cadenced, multiethnic song.

Sounds unheard by many, many played for the first
time,

Salsas and fiestas, symphony connoisseurs closing
their eyes,

in clear ferocity waves of people jumping

to the booming, gliding, swirling, whizzing sounds

of strings and synths and drums and winds and vocals,

abandoning boring busy work and obligations,

the rambunctious, rebellious rockers

chanting, clapping, screaming, and singing along

to the tunes intersecting across all the galactic

highways,

from the winding waters of the Grand Canyon

to the healing forests of Tornebau, from the Milky

Way

to Andromeda

The weaving bridges formed,

and people reached out to hold each other's hands

across the galaxies, feeling each other's souls lining

their palms,

clinging strongly together in unison. The lines

intersected,

the world's stringed together, for just a few moments

in the span of

ten billion years the chaos of every thriving world
ceased.

And in a longing, longing, longing fade, the album
enters into the ether, spirited as sound to be reached
for at anytime, whether flying optimistically across
the stars
or being down, face smudged in the dirt and troubled.
An incalculable number have heard, now and forever,
The band from Andromeda...
The band from Andromeda...
The band...

Saturn Song

If I put my hands out,
I can feel the cold clouds
reciprocating my touch,
a living planet amidst the darkness
of nothingness put on pause.

A familiar loop of sounds fixes
all the brutal winds knotting
and tangling every inch of the planet.
For three millenia,

I am the instrument, I am the key,

I am the lead of this improvised song,

arranging and rearranging,

forming and reforming,

shaping and reshaping

the entirety of this planet

through the sounds from my

compass eyes and motioning fingers,

building little castles of solid rock

along the edgeless spaces,

making geographies out of art

along the bending lines of tonal physics.

Landscapes and architectures
open like fields of endless nature.
Greens and blues sprout through the core
and are laid out along the viewing fringes
until the planet is a place at once
both riddled and familiar.

The winds begin to knot again
as the song comes to a fading end,
and all the sounds, they leave my mind,
and I am alone again. Give me time
while my hands and eyes recharge—
another trance is coming.

WHICH SOULS?

Whose small piece of soul dies
in the timbre of belted elegance?
In the pitch buried beneath themselves
only revealed in some a childish past time,
the voices relent the crossing
of skull and soul, like breathless silence
losing haste to comforts in the brain's attics,
where hundred year old dusty boxes
are fussed open and given time,
where both the voice of the soul
and the listener gain a little piece
of each other. In its place,
a scrapyard cacophony of art is
captured, taken, given, and stolen—
another "eureka!" moment
in life's serenading temples.

BIG BANG JARS

Where bombastic silence always lives—
lack of air, lack of life,
an infinite set of microcosmic tendrils
meshing in a continuous process of genesis.

Like nails scratching concrete,
a convergence occurs—
screams of atoms and particles
overtake the mild airlessness,

elements awkwardly isolate, then gang up,
where there is unnamed noise
in its most cacophonous state
without the senses to absorb it,

like the gloam of a beating heart

felt in a drop of amusia,

another incision of space and time,

the catalyst, a shaky hand.

WHERE THE SONGS GO

A soundbox as big as the universe
holding infinite songs in its place—
every blip and orchestral sketch,
every roar and growl of the planets,
from the mud of distorted thoughts
to the ornate harps glazing the ears
to the fiery ruby blaze of stars.
The soundbox holds them
like a web of weaving fog,
memory unneeded, reconciled
in Schrodinger's parallels,
both songs to dwell on made by others
and songs yet unsung and forgotten—recalled.

Thousands of Years From Now

New hymns are written in nanoseconds

in beeps and blips that'll tell a billion stories.

While the scaffolding of stars

uproars and disturbs the sound barriers,

a trillion creatures mincing their first words together

will bring their undeterred faiths to the forefront,

trilling into the galactic tempest's

subconscious being singing brief hymns to itself.

EUROPA BELLS

The jingling scales resound,
sleep is broken.
The dragons erupt
through the methane ice,
shattering their abode,
wringing out their wings
in an icy dancing aerial display.

They sing the language
of the breathless air,
serpentine sounds that slice
through the silence of space
in a near instant;
too fast for sight or satellite,
Earth's oceans begin to ring.

WEAVING LOVE

Soul strings crawl through every vein in us,
and somewhere in each thin twine of thread
a tune a universe away rings in syncopation
with the heart's rhythm, sharing tears and smiles
reflecting the relating, lonesome
space between intergalactic lovers.

An Underwater Whistle

I whistled underwater

To see

If it would make a sound.

Ripples

Left my lips

And water sang for me.

Her watery waves

Flooded the ocean

As she flooded

Me.

Perpetual,

Her profound

Icy breathing

Drowned out

My final cries.

Breathless,

I disappeared

Into great depths.

Unfathomable foams

Consumed me

As I consumed

Her.

I become

One of her

Countless and nameless drops.

Drifting through infinity

In total

Aquatic anonymity.

I whistled underwater

And now know

That it did make a sound.

RAVENOUS

Split black beak
That I parted
And ate its voice.
Our tongues locked
As I drank its dead voice.
Expressionless eyes
Watched the entire rite.

I gripped my throat,
Transcending voice
Into something between
A newborn's croak
And a scream.
My vile cry
Blankets the land,
Drowning laughter.

I have become

The boisterous blaring

Warning,

Spraying poison

As I scour everything in my path.

Blaring deafening death

That consumed the cosmos.

My vile cry,

Pestilence

That blankets the land,

Drowning laughter.

Sound in Space

How we hear a hearkened sigh,
Heaven hushed her hero knights.
Serpents slither out and die,
Let us fly through frightened heights.

Fabled fawn now floats away,
Falling farther into fear.
Silence fills and silence flays,
Fervent flames burn the pier.

Punching, ploughing through the pyre,
Planets blaze in brazen pride.
Plunging right into the fire,
Death by dragonbreath denied.

Calloused calls and chaos came,

Quiet quakes for coloured plains.

Crystal cobras crowd and crawl,

Crumbling crusts they cry against.

Burning both our time and place,

This is how you hear in space!

A Siren's Sigh

Serenade me,

Take me prisoner.

Carry me on

Haunting notes

Of your echoing voice.

I am the weary seaman

Drifting

On endless waves.

The pathless paths

Of cerulean seas

Lead me

To your side.

Your song floats by

The choppy choir

As you sing

To a sorrowful sky.

Your call is my compass

As my sails

Are made full

With your heaving sigh.

I approach

A melancholy mirage,

Lonely as I am.

Solitude is

My only friend

And we long to dissolve

Into your depths.

Watch us drown

In the timeless

Oceans of Jupiter.

RUMBRA

Do they tell tales

Of the massacre on Mars?

How do they explain

Scars and stains

Of scarlet soil?

If you listen

To their rambles of red—

The dead sing tunes

Heard by moons,

Spilled

By the axe

Of the God of war himself.

Two witnesses,

Oscillate in purity

And discuss your guilt,

Shame

That dissipates

Into the black void.

Dead ones tell no tales,

Red secrets howl in gales.

THE SOUND COLLECTOR

Boisterous bottles

Bellowed on,

Interminably.

Shelves upon shelves

Housed the universe in sound.

To wander

As a blind man does,

To wonder

As a mute fool does.

What remains?

A reduction

To sonic essence,

To describe

In pure poetry.

A volcano's roar,

A lake's whisper,

An ocean's cry—

Volumes

Talking tragedy,

Howling horror and

Screaming sorrow.

The sound collector

Gathered madness,

As a thousand moans

Echoed off

The solitude

Of the inside of their jars.

Sing to the Moon

Her love can

Only breathe at night

Like her

Soft song

To the moon.

Longing for her lover,

One heart to another,

She fills

The midnight air

With suffering song.

Where fiery passions

Do not burn,

Her nocturnal melodies

Are pure,

Are Selfless.

Timeless tomes

Of torment

That echo through

The stillness of night.

Lunar limelight

Drowns the songstress

As her tune

Haunts evermore.

Pouring pain

Into music,

She howls at the moon,

Hoping

He will hear her.

THE PIED PIPER OF PLUTO

Melodic echoes

Reverberate

Across the cosmos.

Vibrating memories

That once

Strung the stars

In a straight line.

Hypnosis that

Gripped the world

And twisted the truth—

What they thought

They knew.

If only

They could

Hold your music

In their hands.

Tunes

Mask the dunes

And blind the fool

Who defies science.

The piper

Serenades the masses

Leading them into

The underworld.

It was his fault

That they forgot

Your name.

The Pied Piper

Made them forget,

Then and later.

Travelling Musician

A planet is

My stage,

Where I perform

For uncommon folk

And stars alike.

Travelling through

Space and time

At the speed of light.

My fans

Screaming for more.

"Encore, encore!"

Hardcore.

The Milky Way galaxy tour

Was legendary,

By the spotlight

Of moonlight.

Alas,

The cosmos has grown

Tired

And this is

My farewell.

I am

Face to face

With a black hole.

My quiet audience is

The incomprehensible enemy.

My music falls

On deaf ears.

Confusing silence guides

The notes I make

That suck

Into the inevitable

Abyss.

I fail

And fall

And I now see

That there was

Never truly any

Sound in space.

The Echo

Sealed in a vacuum,
It vibrated—
Resounding,
Jarring screams
Within a jar.

Mouths ajar—
A childbirth cry,
A murderous moan,
A hateful howl,
And a bloodied bellow.
A simmering cacophonous cocktail
Of sorrow
Whose silence I broke
In ether.

An anticosmic abomination

Raping the silence of stars,

Twas a screeching spear

That tore through order.

And across vast galaxies,

Naught was heard.

Twas a whisper

In an eternal dream

That was quickly forgotten.

The awakening

To silence undisturbed—

Not even an echo was heard.

HYMN TO SATURN

As I lay

On freezing rings,

I feel

The rumblings

And grumblings.

But

Where is *your* voice?

Hearing timeless

Jingles of Jupiter

Hopelessly echo

Through the stars;

Like a forgotten song

Drifting dreamily

Through darkness.

My ears

Are hungry abysses
Waiting for you
To fall into.

Floating aimlessly
In disquietude,
I lay
On freezing rings.
But where is
Your voice?
I am face to face
With my soundless, screaming
Self.

Your moons whisper
Legends
Of your song—
Witnesses
To my transformation.

My dissolution

Is sacrifice

In your honour.

With dying breath,

I speak your name.

I hear

The groaning moans,

That dance

On your winds.

A bellowing

Below,

Heard when I stopped

Listening.

Your vicious muted voice,

Screaming with silence

And perfectly pitched

To the tune

Of pitch.

ABOUT THE AUTHORS

GARRETT CARROLL is a poet, writer, and songwriter living in the densest urban city of North Dakota. His work has previously been published in Utopia Science Fiction, Star*Line Magazine, Aphelion Webzine, and contributes essays and articles to the SFPA blog. He holds a B.A. in English literature from Adams State University.

HAMANT SINGH is a Singaporean writer who is inspired by the Sublime in horror, different cultures and the occult. *Andromeda Dreams* is his fifth release after *The Sibyl* (2002), *CHAOS: Remnants of Ruptured Reflections* (2023) *NÁUSEA / CONFESIÓN* (2023) and *VALTOHA (2024)*.

After a poem was nominated for the 2022 Rhysling Award by the Science Fiction Poetry Association, *The Sibyl* was listed on the preliminary ballot for the 2023 Bram Stoker Awards (Superior Achievement in a Poetry Collection). In 2023, *The Sibyl* was also nominated for the Elgin Award. Hamant currently resides in Guadalajara, Mexico where he is currently working on an art/poetry collaboration with Irish artist Shane Reilly amongst other different projects.

www.ingramcontent.com/pod-product-compliance
Lightning Source LLC
Chambersburg PA
CBHW070452130626
46553CB00006B/2375